FOR YOU

MY LIFE MEMOIR

CURATED BY RIP GERBER

FOR YOU

MY LIFE MEMOIR

Front cover image/book design by VisualPhilosophy.

ISBN: 978-1629671451

Library of Congress Control Number: 2019936128

Gratitude to Tom Addis, Ted Barnett, Rob Birmingham, Dana Bonham, Scott Bonham, Jean-Pierre Conte, Juan Enriquez, Steven Feinberg, John Gaines, Audrey Gerber, James Gutierrez, Russell Jones, Brian Laidlaw, Liz Lyons, Frances Martin, Mark Murphy, Jennifer Raiser, Phillip Raiser, Preston Raisin, Dan Reardon, Eric Ridder, Keri Ridder, Javiar Rojas, Michelle Ross, David Schmaier, Brian Schwartz, John Shuhda, Hillary Thomas, Jono Tunney, Tina Tunney, Eric Upin and Colin Wiel for their ideas, advice and support in creating this book, and to Margaret, Lauren, Lily and Ella for your courage and inspiration, and for sharing your Erik with all of us, forever.

Printed and bound in the United States of America
First Printing April 2019

Published by Wise Media Group, Morro Bay, California

Visit www.ripgerber.com
to learn more of the history and inspiration
behind 'FOR YOU'

One warm June morning, Erik Smith did not wake up.

Devoted husband, loving father, and dear friend to many, Erik was an inspiration and mentor. He taught me and those close to him how to live life and always be present. After an ordinary family dinner and night of watching television with his three daughters, Erik fell asleep on his couch in Tiburon, California. At some moment before dawn, Erik passed away. He was 55, vibrant, full of laughter and light. I loved him like a brother.

Erik's service, held at the Olympic Club in San Francisco, was both solemn and celebratory. The final remembrance was given by Erik's eldest daughters, Lauren and Lily. The girls approached the podium and read from a book Erik secretly kept beside his bed, a private diary where he would capture memories, prescribe advice, scribble favorite quotes and share his deepest feelings. Wise words and favorite sayings from Erik's book were also printed in the Celebration of Life program for the service. So much of Erik was revealed as his daughters read from his secret memoir.

That reading became the inspiration behind the book you now hold. Erik's passing compelled me to write my thoughts down as he did, to create my own book to help me capture more of myself for my family. (As Erik once scribbled: *"Embrace bedtime storytelling."*) And I wanted to share the prompts and questions with Erik's friends and family, so that they too might carry on his thoughtful tradition. Erik would have encouraged me to do just that, so that we could all share more of ourselves. Understanding is a powerful force in deepening our love of one another.

Each of us has an Erik in our lives. Perhaps more than one: a beloved friend or family member who passes, perhaps suddenly without warning, perhaps slowly over time. We want to remember everything we can about those we love. And we hope that they will remember us. This book was created to facilitate more understanding, celebration and love, to capture a glimpse of ourselves, before time runs out.

FOR YOU is dedicated to Erik Smith and his incredible daughters. Proceeds from sales of FOR YOU are donated to the St. Jude's Children's Research Hospital Erik Michael Smith Gift Fund.

I love you, Smitty. You are remembered, forever.

ERIK MICHAEL SMITH

October 28, 1962 – June 20, 2018

———

FOR YOU
MY LIFE MEMOIR

NAME

....

DATE STARTED

....

Whether this book has been given to you or you have gotten it for yourself, this book is for you, for you to discover, capture and share everything about you. FOR YOU is a blank canvas upon which you can document the journey of your incredible life. It is for you to preserve and share the memory of you, for you have an important story to share. FOR YOU is your personal and intimate archive for you to share with those you love. When these questions are completed by you, this book becomes your gift. For you will one day leave behind FOR YOU to those dear to you, those you want to know more of your story and learn more about the answers to your questions. Sharing will help strengthen and build connections between the people you love as they remember you for your journey, your decisions, your accomplishments, your challenges, your beliefs and your dreams. For you will teach in these pages the value of perspective and experiences and living. Your story matters. And that is why FOR YOU is dedicated to you.

How did you come to receive FOR YOU?

....

....

....

Why is FOR YOU in your life at this time?

....

....

....

CONTENTS

CHAPTER 1

MY NAME

FOR YOU

MY NAME

My full name...

....

What my name means..

....

....

How my name was chosen...

....

....

....

Other names I have been called, and why...

....

....

....

Other names I would have picked, or would liked to be called, and why.......................

....

....

....

....

CHAPTER 2

MY TOP 30

FOR YOU

MY TOP 30

1. My favorite moment of my life

2. My best friend of all time

3. The one thing I wish I had done

4. The one thing I wish I had not done

....

....

....

....

....

5. What I stand for

....

....

....

....

6. One talent I wish I had

....

....

....

....

7. My one dream that later came true

8. My greatest achievement

9. My great failure

10. What I want my friends and family to say about me

....

....

....

....

....

11. The purpose of my life

....

....

....

....

12. The most important lesson of all

....

....

....

....

13. My perfect day

....

....

....

....

....

14. My reason for living

....

....

....

....

....

15. The hardest lesson I ever learned

....

....

....

....

....

16. The easiest thing for me to do

17. What love really means

18. The most important question to ask

19. A moment when I experienced complete happiness, and why

20. My values and core beliefs

21. What I have always gotten right

22. What I always seem to get wrong

....

....

....

....

....

23. The apologies I never made but wish I had

....

....

....

....

....

24. My strengths

....

....

....

....

....

25. My weaknesses

....

....

....

....

....

26. What always makes me smile

....

....

....

....

27. The things I know I should be doing, but don't

....

....

....

....

28. How I think I am perceived

....

....

....

....

....

29. The most important thing I still need to accomplish

....

....

....

....

....

30. If I could change anything it would be

....

....

....

....

....

CHAPTER 3

MY CHILDHOOD

FOR YOU

MY CHILDHOOD

My birthday ....

My birthplace ....

How I was born ....

....

....

What was happening in my parents' lives before my birth/adoption ....

....

....

....

What I was told about my baby years ....

....

....

....

My favorite baby story ....

....

....

MY CHILDHOOD

How I ranked in early childhood development:

	Challenging	Average	Advanced	Special Memories
Arithmetic	○	○	○	
Bumping into things	○	○	○	
Colicky	○	○	○	
Eating	○	○	○	
Laughing	○	○	○	
Nursing	○	○	○	
Potty training	○	○	○	
Reading	○	○	○	
Sleeping through the night	○	○	○	
Socializing	○	○	○	
Talking	○	○	○	
Teething	○	○	○	
Walking	○	○	○	
Writing	○	○	○	

MY CHILDHOOD

My most unique personality traits as a child ....

....

....

....

....

The object I was most emtionally attached to as a child ....

....

....

....

....

I called that special object ....

....

....

....

....

MY CHILDHOOD

Who influenced me most as a child, and why ....

....

....

....

....

....

....

....

Who I wanted to be like when I grew up, and why ....

....

....

....

....

....

....

....

My childhood activities included

	Never	Occasionally	Loved it	Special Memories
Amusment parks, carnivals and fairs	○	○	○	
Arts and crafts	○	○	○	
Attending live performances (concerts, plays, shows)	○	○	○	
Attending sporting events	○	○	○	
Birthday parties	○	○	○	
Board games	○	○	○	
Building things	○	○	○	
Computer time	○	○	○	
Creating imaginary places/events	○	○	○	
Exercising	○	○	○	
Getting gifts	○	○	○	
Giving gifts	○	○	○	
Going to restaurants	○	○	○	
Inventing things	○	○	○	
Napping	○	○	○	
Playing in the snow	○	○	○	
Playing inside	○	○	○	

My childhood activities included *(continued)*

	Never	Occasionally	Loved it	Special Memories
Playing outside	○	○	○	
Playing sports	○	○	○	
Playing with friends	○	○	○	
Reading	○	○	○	
Shopping with adults	○	○	○	
Singing	○	○	○	
Studying	○	○	○	
Swimming	○	○	○	
Talking on the phone	○	○	○	
Tinkering and electronics	○	○	○	
Travelling	○	○	○	
Visiting museums	○	○	○	
Walking and hiking	○	○	○	
Watching TV, movies, sports	○	○	○	
Word games and cosswords	○	○	○	
Writing	○	○	○	
Other?	○	○	○	

MY CHILDHOOD

My earliest childhood memories

The childhood home I enjoyed the most

The first schools I attended

MY CHILDHOOD

My fondest memory from my early school days ....

....

....

....

....

My favorite family vacation or trip as a child ....

....

....

....

....

My favorite foods, snacks and treats growing up

My favorite, and least favorite, chores around the house ....

....

....

....

....

MY CHILDHOOD

The time I got into trouble as a child ....

....

....

....

....

My favorite toy or game growing up ....

....

....

....

....

My favorite TV, radio show or movie growing up ....

....

....

....

My favorite books growing up ....

....

....

....

MY CHILDHOOD

My first childhood memory ....

....

....

....

....

....

My favorite pet, and why ....

....

....

....

....

....

My favorite teacher from my childhood, and why ....

....

....

....

....

....

MY CHILDHOOD

My most memorable birthday as a child

....

....

....

....

....

My favorite holiday as a child

....

....

....

....

My favorite family traditions as a child

....

....

....

....

Other memories from my childhood

CHAPTER 4

MY
TEEN YEARS

FOR YOU

My best friend/s in high school, and why ....

....

....

....

....

As a teenager, I would describe myself as ....

....

....

....

....

My teenage personality traits ....

....

....

....

....

MY TEEN YEARS

As a teenager, my high school friends would describe me as ....

....

....

....

....

After school, I would typically ....

....

....

....

....

The most trouble I ever got into as a teenager ....

....

....

....

....

....

MY TEEN YEARS

The nicest thing I ever did as a teenager ....

....

....

....

....

....

The teen years presented me with some tough choices.

My attitudes towards drinking, smoking, reckless behavior, and testing the limits were ....

....

....

....

....

....

....

My favorite memory as a teenager ....

....

....

....

MY TEEN YEARS

My funniest teenage moment ....
....
....
....
....

As a teenager, I always thought I would grow up to be a ....

because ....
....
....
....

As a teenager .... had the biggest (positive/negative)

influence on me, because ....
....
....
....
....

MY TEEN YEARS

Growing up, to earn money, I did chores and odd jobs, including

My favorite memories growing up as a teenager in my home

My favorite vacation as a teenager

MY TEEN YEARS

Some of my heros as a teenager ....

....

....

....

....

....

Growing up, the one fashion article or accessory that I identified with, that I wore most often

....

....

....

....

....

My favorite and least favorite subjects in high school ....

....

....

....

....

....

MY TEEN YEARS

My most memorable school project ....

....

....

....

....

....

The first car I ever drove ....

....

....

....

As a teenager, I stood out in several ways. I was mostly known for ....

....

....

....

....

....

....

MY TEEN YEARS

A romantic relationship in my teenage years was with ....

How we met, and some of the things we did together, include ....

....

....

....

....

....

My first kiss ....

....

....

....

....

....

Growing up I mostly listened to .... **music.**

My favorite artists, albums, and songs include ....

....

....

....

My favorite quotes and sayings growing up ....

....

....

....

....

....

....

....

The most awkward moment of my youth ....

....

....

....

....

....

....

....

....

Memories I'd like to forget

CHAPTER 5

MY
FAVORITE
THINGS

FOR YOU

MY FAVORITE THINGS

My favorite and lucky numbers ....

....

My favorite kind of pet is a .... , and the most beloved pet from my life is

....

....

My favorite foods ....

....

....

My favorite sports and teams to watch ....

....

....

My favorite physical activities and sports to play ....

....

....

My favorite place to vacation ....

....

....

My favorite city in the world ....

MY FAVORITE THINGS

My favorite drink to share with others...

....

....

My favorite book...

....

....

My favorite song of all time...

....

....

My favorite movie of all time...

....

....

My favorite actor/actress...

....

....

My favorite motto, quote or saying..

....

....

MY FAVORITE THINGS

My favorite color..

My favorite animals...

....

....

My favorite perfume or cologne..

....

....

My favorite relax and 'lounge around' outfit...

....

....

My favorite signature accessory or piece of clothing that is uniquely me...........................

....

....

My favorite piece of jewelry...

....

My favorite time of year..

....

My favorite time of day...

MY FAVORITE THINGS

My other favorite things..

....

....

....

....

....

....

....

....

....

....

....

....

....

....

....

....

CHAPTER 6

MY
BLOODLINE

FOR YOU

MY BLOODLINE

The names of my mother, father, siblings and other close relatives...

....

....

....

....

My mother grew up in...

Some of my favorite stories she shared of her youth..

....

....

....

....

My father grew up in..

Some of my favorite stories he shared of his youth...

....

....

....

....

MY BLOODLINE

My mother's occupations

My father's occupations

One thing I inherited from my mother

MY BLOODLINE

One thing I inherited from my father

_____

_____

_____

_____

My fondest memory of my mother

_____

_____

_____

_____

My fondest memory of my father

_____

_____

_____

_____

_____

MY BLOODLINE

The three things I love most about my mother

....

....

....

....

....

The three things I love most about my father

....

....

....

....

....

My mother believed in

....

....

....

....

....

MY BLOODLINE

My father believed in

One thing I always wished for about my mother

One thing I always wished for about my father

MY BLOODLINE

The most important lesson I learned from my mother

....

....

....

....

....

The most important lesson I learned from my father

....

....

....

....

....

My mother's side of the family

....

....

....

....

....

MY BLOODLINE

My father's side of the family ....

....

....

....

....

....

When growing up, I called my parents ....

....

....

....

....

My parents met in ....

They met because ....

....

....

....

MY BLOODLINE

My parents were married/unionized in ....

....

....

....

....

....

When I was growing up, my parents' relationship was ....

....

....

....

....

The most important lesson I learned from my parents' relationship ....

....

....

....

....

MY BLOODLINE

My favorite and most memorable aunts, uncles and cousins

My favorite stories about my family

My most famous relative or ancestor

MY BLOODLINE

My family is somewhat famous for ....

....

....

....

....

....

The one person in my family who was wild or downright crazy ....

....

....

....

....

....

The family member I most admired growing up ....

....

....

....

....

....

Some of the family legends or stories I recall ....

....

....

....

....

....

My godparents, and why my parents picked them ....

....

....

....

One family secret I would want passed along to future generations ....

....

....

....

....

MY BLOODLINE

More about my heritage

CHAPTER 7

MY FAMILY

FOR YOU

MY FAMILY

PARTNER/MARRIAGE

Name

When and where we got engaged/got married

Our ceremony and activities included

PARTNER/MARRIAGE

Name

When and where we got engaged/got married

Our ceremony and activities included

PARTNER/MARRIAGE

Name

When and where we got engaged/got married

Our ceremony and activities included

Our honeymoon/special vacation was to ....

and we ....

....

....

....

....

My partner means many things to me, such as ....

....

....

....

....

....

The qualities I love most in my partner are ....

....

....

....

....

....

MY FAMILY

I met my partner on/at *(date/place)* ....

....

What first attracted me to my current partner ....

....

....

....

....

....

....

Goals my partner and I have made together, and accomplished together ....

....

....

....

....

....

....

....

MY FAMILY

Goals my partner and I still want to pursue and achieve together

....

....

....

....

....

....

....

....

My favorite memories of how we met

....

....

....

....

....

....

....

My favorite memories of our engagement and marriage

Some of the people in our wedding ceremony, and why they were included

One moment in our wedding ceremony I will always cherish

....

....

....

....

....

....

Our newlywed life could best described as

....

....

....

....

....

....

....

....

CHILDREN

Name ....

Birthday ....

Birth place ....

Natural/Adopted ....

Named after ....

Name ....

Birthday ....

Birth place ....

Natural/Adopted ....

Named after ....

Name ....

Birthday ....

Birth place ....

Natural/Adopted ....

Named after ....

Name ....

Birthday ....

Birth place ....

Natural/Adopted ....

Named after ....

Name ....

Birthday ....

Birth place ....

Natural/Adopted ....

Named after ....

Name ....

Birthday ....

Birth place ....

Natural/Adopted ....

Named after ....

MY FAMILY

The most challenging parenting aspect for each of my children

....

....

....

....

....

....

....

....

What makes me the proudest about each of my children

....

....

....

....

....

....

....

MY FAMILY

One memorable moment about each of my children

....

....

....

....

....

....

....

....

A special word or phrase I shared with each of my children

....

....

....

....

....

....

....

MY FAMILY

Famous quote that best defines or describes each of my children...

....

....

....

....

....

....

....

One of my favorite family vacations...

....

....

....

....

....

....

....

....

....

MY FAMILY

My favorite family pets were (name/breed/time period/reason) ....

....

....

....

....

....

....

....

One of my favorite 'pet memories' ....

....

....

....

....

....

....

....

MY FAMILY

My family traditions that I hope to continue

CHAPTER 8

MY IFs

FOR YOU

MY IFs

If I won a $10m lottery, I would ....

....

....

....

....

....

If I could change anything in my life it would be ....

....

....

....

....

If one dream came true it would be ....

....

....

....

....

....

MY IFs

If I could go back to any period in time, I would go back to ....

....

....

....

....

....

If I suddenly became famous, it would be for ....

....

....

....

....

....

If I had more time, I would ....

....

....

....

....

....

MY IFs

If I could have dinner with a famous person, dead or alive, it would be ....

....

....

....

....

If I could ask God one question, it would be ....

....

....

....

....

If I could change one decision in my life, it would be ....

....

....

....

....

MY IFs

If I could live anywhere else in the world, it would be ....

because ....

....

....

....

....

If I could be reincarnated as any animal, my 'spirit animal', I would be a ....

because ....

....

....

....

....

....

....

....

....

....

CHAPTER 9

MY
FRIENDS

FOR YOU

The three traits I seek in a close friend

The friends I've had for the longest time, and why

My old friend I miss the most

MY FRIENDS

My friend that makes me laugh the most ....

....

My friend I can tell anything to ....

....

My friend who has always given me the best advice ....

....

My friend I have had the most adventures with ....

....

My friend who challenges me the most ....

....

Five (5) friends and the attributes I admire most about each ....

....

....

....

....

....

....

....

....

MY FRIENDS

My friends I've lost along the way, and why I miss them ....

....

....

....

....

The friends I would invite to a dinner party in my honor, and why ....

....

....

....

....

....

My best friend as a child ....

....

....

My best friend as a teenager ....

....

....

MY FRIENDS

My best friend as an adult ....

....

....

....

....

The one friend I would want to attend my funeral service that might surprise others ....

....

....

....

....

....

The one thing I never said to my closest friends that I wanted to ....

....

....

....

....

....

....

CHAPTER 10

MY
LOOK

FOR YOU

MY LOOK

As of *(date)*... my height, weight, and distinguishing features are

height ....

weight ....

distinguishing features ....

....

The one thing I can do with my voice or body that I'm really good at ....

....

....

The health issues, surgeries and illnesses I have endured ....

....

....

....

....

The scars I have and how I got them ....

....

....

....

The one odd thing I can do with my body that most people cannot do ....

....

MY LOOK

Some of my most distinguishing mannerisms...

....

....

....

....

My favorite clothes to wear...

....

....

....

Why I wear my hair the way I do...

....

....

My famous 'looks' through the years...

....

....

....

How others would describe my appearance...

....

....

My best attempt at a self-portrait

MY LOOK

Other ways I describe myself ....

....

....

....

....

....

....

....

....

....

....

....

....

....

....

....

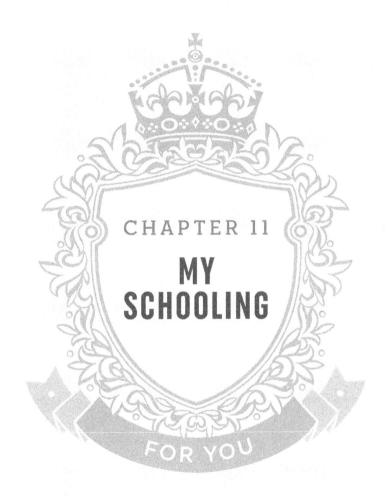

CHAPTER 11

MY
SCHOOLING

FOR YOU

MY SCHOOLING

My favorite time in school was at..

....

because...

....

....

....

My least favorite time in school was at..

....

because...

....

....

....

My most memoriable school experience was...

....

....

....

MY SCHOOLING

The most famous mistake I made during my education..

....

....

....

....

The school/s I applied to but did not go to..

....

....

....

The reasons I attended the schools I did..

....

....

....

....

The easiest thing about school for me...

....

....

....

....

MY SCHOOLING

The hardest thing about school for me ....

....

....

....

My favorite subjects and courses ....

....

....

....

My least favorite subjects and courses ....

....

....

....

I would describe my study habits as ....

....

....

....

MY SCHOOLING

The teacher that influenced me the most was ....

at ....

because ....

....

....

....

The clubs and organizations I most enjoyed most at school ....

....

....

....

....

....

The most important thing I ever learned in school ....

....

....

....

....

....

....

MY SCHOOLING

My favorite activities, sports or clubs in school include

My awards or recognition - good and bad - in my school years include

The diplomas and degrees I received

MY SCHOOLING

The languages I tried to learn to speak

My honest thoughts about the education I received

CHAPTER 12

MY WORK

FOR YOU

MY WORK

My first paying job was as a ....

working for ....

My pay was ....

for doing ....

The lessons I learned on my first job ....

....

....

....

I would describe my work ethic as ....

....

....

....

Some of my favorite jobs growing up ....

....

....

....

....

....

MY WORK

Early in my work career, I found that I had abilities and skills in

Some of the companies and people I have worked for in my life include

The reason I ended up having a career in is because

MY WORK

I retired, or hope to retire in .... and spend my time

....

....

....

Over my career, I have excelled at ....

....

....

....

When meeting strangers, I summarize my work and career as ....

....

....

....

....

What I really want to answer when someone asks 'What do you do?' ....

....

....

....

....

MY WORK

More about my work..

....

....

....

....

....

....

....

....

....

....

....

....

....

....

....

....

CHAPTER 13

MY
SERVICE

FOR YOU

MY SERVICE

My military, government or charity service *(branch of service, enlistment date, discharge date)*

....

....

....

....

My posts *(postings, unit, title, dates, description)*...

....

....

....

....

The reason I decided to join ....

....

....

....

What I enjoyed most about my service ....

....

....

....

MY SERVICE

What I liked least about my service ....

....

....

....

....

....

Some of the most memorable people in my service career ....

....

....

....

....

The five people I would want in my bunker ....

....

....

....

....

....

MY SERVICE

The impact my service had on me ....

....

....

....

My advice to anyone thinking of joining a service organization ....

....

....

The important lessons I learned from my time serving include ....

....

....

The way I truly feel about those institutions I served in ....

....

....

....

My most cherished volunteer projects or time spent was on..

....

....

....

MY SERVICE

More about my service

CHAPTER 14

MY THREE THINGS

FOR YOU

MY THREE THINGS

My three best qualities

1. ....
2. ....
3. ....

Three words that others use to describe me

1. ....
2. ....
3. ....

My three worst attributes

1. ....
2. ....
3. ....

The three words I wish they'd use

1. ....
2. ....
3. ....

The three physical attributes I admire
most about myself

1. ....
2. ....
3. ....

The three moments in my life I am most
ashamed of

1. ....
2. ....
3. ....

MY THREE THINGS

Three people who most changed me

1. ....

2. ....

3. ....

The three most embarrassing things about me

1. ....

2. ....

3. ....

The three words/phrases I use most

1. ....

2. ....

3. ....

The three things I love most about my life

1. ....

2. ....

3. ....

Three moments in my life I'm most proud of

1. ....

2. ....

3. ....

Three things I disslike the most about my life

1. ....

2. ....

3. ....

MY THREE THINGS

The three people, dead or alive, that I consider to be the greatest ever

1. ....
2. ....
3. ....

The three most attractive people in the world today

1. ....
2. ....
3. ....

The three inventions that amaze me the most

1. ....
2. ....
3. ....

My three favorite phases I like to use

1. ....
2. ....
3. ....

My three favorite toys or games

1. ....
2. ....
3. ....

My three favorite words I like to use

1. ....
2. ....
3. ....

MY THREE THINGS

The three most significant historical events that have occurred during my lifetime

1. ....

2. ....

3. ....

The three tools, appliances or machines that are most useful to me in my daily life

1. ....

2. ....

3. ....

The three lessons I've learned in my life

1. ....

2. ....

3. ....

The three happiest moments in my life

1. ....

2. ....

3. ....

The three things I would never do

1. ....

2. ....

3. ....

My three favorite charities I support

1. ....

2. ....

3. ....

MY THREE THINGS

The three things I fear the most

1. ....

2. ....

3. ....

My three favorite books

1. ....

2. ....

3. ....

My three favorite songs

1. ....

2. ....

3. ....

The three things I am most grateful for

1. ....

2. ....

3. ....

My three favorite places in the world

1. ....

2. ....

3. ....

My three favorite works of art

1. ....

2. ....

3. ....

MY THREE THINGS

The three truths in this world

1. ....

2. ....

3. ....

The three qualities everyone should possess

1. ....

2. ....

3. ....

The three wishes I want granted

1. ....

2. ....

3. ....

The three things I love most about my life

1. ....

2. ....

3. ....

**The three things that I find most appealing
in the opposite sex**

1. ....

2. ....

3. ....

**The three virtues I believe are the
most important**

1. ....

2. ....

3. ....

CHAPTER 15

MY
SECRETS

FOR YOU

MY SECRETS

Things I keep by my bedside table ....

....

....

....

....

....

Something that I have that nobody knows about ....

....

....

....

....

What I usually wear when I go to bed ....

....

....

....

....

MY SECRETS

If I could afford it, the one thing I would buy that I've always wanted ....

....

....

....

....

....

My strangest possession ....

....

....

....

....

Something or someone I have secretly obsessed over ....

....

....

....

....

MY SECRETS

My pet peeves or triggers that upset or anger me ....

....

....

....

....

....

If my house was burning and I had time to grab only one thing from my possessions, it would be .

....

....

....

....

The time I was caught doing something I should not have been doing ....

....

....

....

....

MY SECRETS

Something forbidden I have done that would surprise even my closest friends

The time I was completely out of control

My most secret passion in life, and why

MY SECRETS

The most romantic date or moment I've ever experienced

....

....

....

....

....

The most appropriate age for someone to begin having sex

....

....

....

....

....

Something everyone thinks is true about me which I know is not

....

....

....

....

....

MY SECRETS

How old I was when I first kissed ....

....

....

....

Something that I have stolen that was not worth the risk ....

....

....

....

The person that I have fantasized most about in my thoughts ....

....

....

....

....

One thing in the world that I am addicted to ....

....

....

....

....

The wildest party I ever went to ....

....

....

....

....

The drug or alcohol that I once took too much of, and why ....

....

....

....

....

The biggest risk I've ever taken where I narrowly escaped death or put my physical self in

harm's way ....

....

....

....

....

MY SECRETS

If there were no side efects, I would enjoy being addicted to ....

....

....

....

My secret fetish ....

....

....

....

My ultimate fantasy is ....

....

....

....

....

....

The secret to a happy life is ....

....

....

....

MY SECRETS

The time I was in a physical fight, how it happened and how I fared ....

....

....

....

....

My secret tickle spots ....

....

....

....

....

The biggest thrill I've ever experienced, and why ....

....

....

....

....

....

....

....

....

MY SECRETS

My other secrets

CHAPTER 16

MY
BELIEFS

FOR YOU

MY BELIEFS

My religious affiliation ....

....

....

....

My parent's religious affiliation ....

....

....

....

I describe my God as ....

....

....

....

....

....

MY BELIEFS

My religious rites (name, location, date, officiant, sponsors/witnesses) ....

....

....

....

My religious rites (name, location, date, officiant, sponsors/witnesses) ....

....

....

....

My religious rites (name, location, date, officiant, sponsors/witnesses) ....

....

....

....

My religious rites (name, location, date, officiant, sponsors/witnesses) ....

....

....

....

....

MY BELIEFS

How my beliefs have evolved over the years ....

....

....

....

....

....

A religion that to me is the strangest ....

....

....

....

....

How often I attend religious services, and why ....

....

....

....

....

How I picture the world a thousand years from now ....

....

....

....

....

....

The time God spoke to me, and what the conversation was about ....

....

....

....

....

....

My superstitious habits, actions and beliefs ....

....

....

....

....

....

What I believed a spiritual guide/pyschic/clairavoyent once told me, and the most shocking part was ....

....

....

....

....

What was shared by someone that I thought was truly unbelievable ....

....

....

....

....

The political topics that I believe in the most ....

....

....

....

....

MY BELIEFS

The social issues I care about the most ....

....

....

....

....

....

My political affiliation is ....

because ....

....

....

....

How I would solve world hunger ....

....

....

....

....

....

How I would end poverty in my country ....

....

....

....

....

....

The most important environmental problem is ....

and I would solve it by ....

....

....

....

Something I believe in that I wish more people did too ....

....

....

....

....

....

MY BELIEFS

More of my beliefs

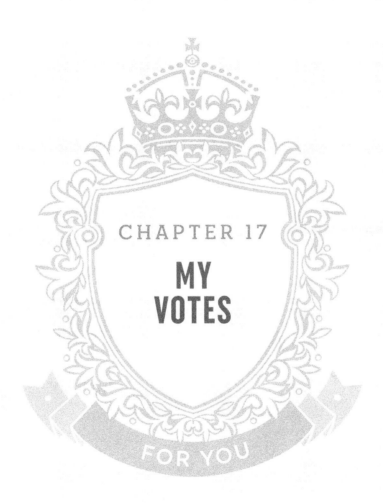

CHAPTER 17

MY
VOTES

FOR YOU

MY VOTES

	Yes	No
Women have the right to have an abortion	○	○
Citizens have the right to own guns	○	○
My country should impose the death penalty	○	○
Marijuana should be legal	○	○
Homosexuals should have the same rights as heterosexuals	○	○
Global warming is a real threat	○	○
I keep a diary	○	○
I exercise regularly	○	○
I recycle batteries properly	○	○
I snore	○	○
I remember jokes	○	○
I remember people's names	○	○
There is a God	○	○
There is a heaven and a hell	○	○

	Yes	No
Life exists elsewhere in the universe	○	○
Aliens or other life forms have made contact with us	○	○
Humans evolved from apes	○	○
Astrology is real and predictive	○	○
I read my horoscope	○	○
I believe my horoscope	○	○
I am superstitous	○	○
I believe in the afterlife	○	○
I believe in reincarnation	○	○
I have seen a spiritual guide, pyschic or clairavoyant	○	○
I take advice from total strangers	○	○
I always tip for good service	○	○
I am always on time	○	○
I've spent the night outdoors	○	○

MY VOTES

	Yes	No		Yes	No
I believe in karma	○	○	Same sex marriage should be legal	○	○
It's OK to break the law sometimes	○	○	Markets need more regulatory oversight	○	○
Money can buy happiness	○	○	All animals have rights	○	○
I've struggled more than most	○	○	I know my life's purpose	○	○
Technology is good for mankind	○	○	Nothing really changes	○	○
I've stolen money from my parents	○	○	I have broken someone's heart	○	○
Less is more	○	○	Why wouldn't we	○	○
I have fired a gun	○	○	An eye for an eye	○	○
I have hunted and killed an animal	○	○	Women are more powerful than men	○	○
I have given blood	○	○	I have found my soul mate	○	○
I know what I am here for	○	○	Taxes should be increased	○	○
I give money to the homeless	○	○	I feel vulnerable sharing so much	○	○
Life has treated me well	○	○	There is no such thing as luck	○	○
I have no regrets	○	○	My destiny is predetermined	○	○
People are good	○	○	I always play by the rules	○	○

CHAPTER 18

MY
STUFF

FOR YOU

The favorite places I have lived: (address, occupants/co-owners, dates)

MY STUFF

The favorite places I have lived: (address, occupants/co-owners, dates)

MY STUFF

I would describe my favorite home as ....

....

....

....

....

....

My fondest memory of a place I have lived is ....

....

....

....

....

....

The first car I ever drove or bought ....

....

....

My driving record is ....

....

....

MY STUFF

One of the worst accidents I had in my home or car was ....

....

....

....

....

....

My most expensive possessions I have ever owned include ....

....

....

....

....

My most prized possession ....

....

....

....

....

....

MY STUFF

Some of the things I have collected in my life, and why ....

....

....

....

....

....

....

My family heirlooms, and why they are important to me ....

....

....

....

....

Musical instruments I learned to play, and why ....

....

....

....

MY STUFF

Gifts I have received that I will always treasure...

....

....

....

....

....

....

Some of my favorite hobbies, and why...

....

....

....

....

....

....

....

....

....

....

MY STUFF

The most expensive thing I have ever owned ....

....

....

....

....

Some things I still keep, even though they are not valuable ....

....

....

....

....

The one thing I own that defines who I am ....

....

....

....

....

....

MY STUFF

The one thing I have lost that I wish I still had

My favorite tool or appliance, and why

How much I think I am worth now

The contents of my wallet or purse include

MY STUFF

My favorite pair of shoes, and what they say about me ....

....

....

....

....

If I suddenly received a million dollars, I would spend it on ....

....

....

....

....

Something I would never buy or own, even if I had plenty of money ....

....

....

....

....

MY STUFF

More of my stuff

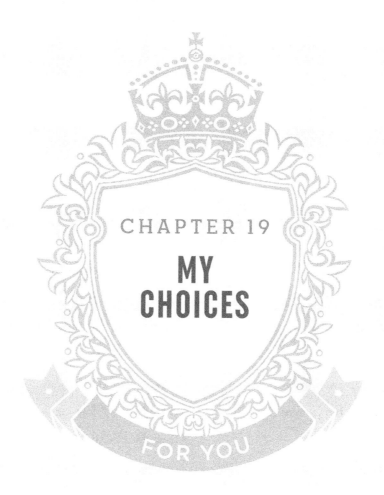

CHAPTER 19

MY CHOICES

FOR YOU

MY CHOICES

Adventurous ○ or Cautious ○

Amusement Park ○ or Day at the Beach ○

Antique ○ or Brand New ○

Apples ○ or Oranges ○

Asking Questions ○ or Answering Questions ○

Bagels ○ or Muffins ○

Baseball ○ or Basketball ○

Bath ○ or Shower ○

Beads ○ or Pearls ○

Beatles ○ or Rolling Stones ○

Beer ○ or Wine ○

Big Party ○ or Small Gathering ○

Black ○ or White ○

Black Leather ○ or Brown Leather ○

Board Games ○ or Video Games ○

Bond ○ or Bourne ○

Book ○ or eBook ○

Books ○ or Movies ○

Boots ○ or Sandals ○

Bracelet ○ or Necklace ○

Briefs ○ or Boxers ○

Bull ○ or Bear ○

Cake ○ or Pie ○

Email ○ or Text ○

Car ○ or Truck ○

Card Game ○ or Board Game ○

Cardio ○ or Weights ○

Cats ○ or Dogs ○

Checkers ○ or Chess ○

Chinese ○ or Italian ○

Chocolate ○ or Vanilla ○

City ○ or Country ○

Classical Art ○ or Modern Art ○

Coffee ○ or Tea ○

Coke ○ or Pepsi ○

Comedy ○ or Mystery ○

Crossword Puzzle ○ or Sudoku ○

Dancing ○ or Singing ○

Democrat ○ or Republican ○

Cook ○ or Delivery ○

Dry ○ or Wet ○

Drawings ○ or Paintings ○

MY CHOICES

Dress Up ◯ or Dress Down ◯

Dresses ◯ or Skirts ◯

Early Bird ◯ or Night Owl ◯

Facial Hair ◯ or Clean Shaven ◯

Fair ◯ or Theme Park ◯

Fame ◯ or Fortune ◯

Fiction ◯ or Non-fiction ◯

Football ◯ or Soccer ◯

Form ◯ or Function ◯

Fruit ◯ or Vegetables ◯

Glasses ◯ or Contacts ◯

Grammys ◯ or Oscars ◯

Hamburger ◯ or Taco ◯

Hardwood ◯ or Carpet ◯

Heaven ◯ or Earth ◯

Honesty ◯ or Others' Feelings ◯

Honey Mustard ◯ or BBQ Sauce ◯

Hugs ◯ or Kisses ◯

Hunting ◯ or Fishing ◯

Ice Cream ◯ or Yogurt ◯

Iced Coffee ◯ or Hot Coffee ◯

Introvert ◯ or Extrovert ◯

iOS ◯ or Android ◯

Jazz ◯ or Classical ◯

Jello ◯ or Pudding ◯

Jesus ◯ or Buddha ◯

Jogging ◯ or Hiking ◯

Ketchup ◯ or Mustard ◯

Long Hair ◯ or Short Hair ◯

MAC ◯ or PC ◯

Man ◯ or Woman ◯

Marvel ◯ or DC ◯

Meat ◯ or Vegetables ◯

Mom ◯ or Dad ◯

Movie at Home ◯ or Movie at the Theater ◯

Movie Candy ◯ or Movie Popcorn ◯

Multiple Choice Questions ◯ or Essay Questions ◯

Numbers ◯ or Letters ◯

Ocean ◯ or Mountains ◯

Oreos ◯ or Chips Ahoy ◯

Pancake ◯ or Waffle ◯

Passenger ◯ or Driver ◯

MY CHOICES

Peanut Butter ◯ or Jelly ◯

Pen ◯ or Pencil ◯

Personal Chef ◯ or Personal Trainer ◯

Pizza ◯ or Pasta ◯

Pro-choice ◯ or Pro-life ◯

Raisins ◯ or Nuts ◯

Ready, Aim, Fire ◯ or Ready, Fire, Aim ◯

Rich Friend ◯ or Loyal Friend ◯

Roller Coaster ◯ or Ferris Wheel ◯

Rural ◯ or Urban ◯

Sausage ◯ or Bacon ◯

Saver ◯ or Spender ◯

Sci-Fi ◯ or Fantasy ◯

Scrambled ◯ or Fried ◯

Silver ◯ or Gold ◯

Skiing ◯ or Snowboarding ◯

Sky Dive ◯ or Bungee Jump ◯

Smoking ◯ or Non-smoking

Snakes ◯ or Sharks ◯

Sneakers ◯ or Sandals ◯

Soup ◯ or Sandwich ◯

Spicy ◯ or Mild ◯

Spring ◯ or Fall ◯

Star Wars ◯ or Star Trek ◯

Stripes ◯ or Solids ◯

Sunrises ◯ or Sunsets ◯

Sweater ◯ or Hoodie ◯

Swimming ◯ or Sunbathing ◯

Tattoos ◯ or Piercings ◯

Train ◯ or Plane ◯

Truth ◯ or Dare ◯

TV Shows ◯ or Movies ◯

Washing Dishes ◯ or Doing Laundry ◯

Whole Wheat ◯ or White ◯

Wine ◯ or Beer ◯

Winter ◯ or Summer ◯

Work Hard ◯ or Play Hard ◯

Working Alone ◯ or Working in a Team ◯

.... ◯ or ....

.... ◯ or ....

.... ◯ or ....

.... ◯ or ....

MY CHOICES

My other choices

CHAPTER 20

MY
MEMORIES

FOR YOU

MY MEMORIES

For me memories are best described as ....

....

....

....

....

....

The memory I wish to pass onto others ....

....

....

....

....

....

A moment in my life I will never forget ....

....

....

....

....

MY MEMORIES

My most vivid memory

....

....

....

....

....

Something that scared me most

....

....

....

....

The most hilarious moment of my life

....

....

....

....

....

MY MEMORIES

The first person I fell in love with was...

and it happened because...

....

....

....

....

....

The first time I ever earned money it made me feel..

....

....

....

....

Someone in my life who was incredibly kind to me...

....

....

....

....

The longest grudge I've ever held, and why

....

....

....

....

....

The most peaceful moment in my life

....

....

....

....

The most tragic moment of my life

....

....

....

....

....

MY MEMORIES

Things I always remember

Things I always forget

Something I want to forget

An act of kindness I would like to be remembered for

MY MEMORIES

More of my memories ....

....

....

....

....

....

....

....

....

....

....

....

....

....

....

....

....

CHAPTER 21

MY
BUCKET
LIST

FOR YOU

MY BUCKET LIST

	Did it	Want to do it	Would never do it
Achieve my ideal body weight	○	○	○
Act in a film	○	○	○
Appear on TV	○	○	○
Attend a major sports event	○	○	○
Attend the Olympics	○	○	○
Bungy jump	○	○	○
Chase a tornado or storm	○	○	○
Climb a mountain	○	○	○
Connect with a past teacher	○	○	○
Create my family tree	○	○	○
Do volunteer work	○	○	○
Donate blood	○	○	○
Eat an insect	○	○	○
Eat at a 5-Star restaurant	○	○	○
Explore a cave	○	○	○
Fight with my fists	○	○	○
Fly in a helicopter	○	○	○
Fly in a hot air balloon	○	○	○
Fly in a private jet	○	○	○
Get a tatoo	○	○	○
Give to a charity anonymously	○	○	○

MY BUCKET LIST

	Did it	Want to do it	Would never do it.
Go backpacking/camping	○	○	○
Go deep sea fishing	○	○	○
Go horseback riding	○	○	○
Go on a blind date	○	○	○
Go on a cruise	○	○	○
Go on a safari	○	○	○
Go skydiving	○	○	○
Go streaking	○	○	○
Go surfing	○	○	○
Go whale watching	○	○	○
Go white water rafting	○	○	○
Grow something in a garden	○	○	○
Have an out-of-body experience	○	○	○
Have my portrait painted	○	○	○
Helio-skiing	○	○	○
Juggle	○	○	○
Jury duty	○	○	○
Learn a new language	○	○	○
Learn to play a musical instrument	○	○	○
Make a difference in a stranger's life	○	○	○
Meet the President or a top government official	○	○	○

MY BUCKET LIST

	Did it	Want to do it	Would never do it.
Mentor someone	○	○	○
Observe a falling star	○	○	○
Participate in an extreme sport	○	○	○
Pet a snake	○	○	○
Plant a tree	○	○	○
Publish a book	○	○	○
Ride a bull	○	○	○
Ride a roller coaster	○	○	○
Ride an elephant	○	○	○
Ride in a hot-air balloon	○	○	○
Run a marathon	○	○	○
Scuba dive	○	○	○
See the Grand Canyon	○	○	○
See the Mona Lisa	○	○	○
See the Northern Lights	○	○	○
Send a message in a bottle	○	○	○
Shower in a waterfall	○	○	○
Sing in front of an audience	○	○	○
Ski (snow, water)	○	○	○
Skinny dip	○	○	○

MY BUCKET LIST

	Did it	Want to do it	Would never do it.
Skydive	○	○	○
Sleep in a castle	○	○	○
Sleep under the stars	○	○	○
Smoke a cigar	○	○	○
Speak in public	○	○	○
Start a business	○	○	○
Swim with dolphins	○	○	○
Swim with sharks	○	○	○
Take an experimental drug	○	○	○
Throw a party for over 100 people	○	○	○
Tour the White House	○	○	○
Visit all seven continents	○	○	○
Walk the Great Wall of China	○	○	○
Wine tasting	○	○	○
Witness a miracle	○	○	○
Witness a solar eclipse	○	○	○
Write a poem	○	○	○
....	○	○	○
....	○	○	○

MY BUCKET LIST

More on my list

MY BUCKET LIST

More on my list

CHAPTER 22

MY
LISTS

FOR YOU

List of things I still need to get done, both big or small

MY LISTS

List of the people I'd like to have attend my funeral

List of all of my favorite food and drink

MY LISTS

List of all the places I've been

List of all of the places I've always wanted to go ....

....

....

....

....

....

....

....

....

....

....

....

....

....

....

....

....

....

List of the most joyful moments and memories of my life ....

....

....

....

....

....

....

....

....

....

....

....

....

....

....

....

....

....

List of all of the things I've always wanted to do

List of the details of what a perfect day is for me

List of the most eccentric facts or trivia that I know that most don't..

....

....

....

....

....

....

....

....

....

....

....

....

....

....

....

....

....

List of all the things I've ever failed at

List of the things that have always bothered me about myself (physical, emotional, social,

spiritual, economic, etc.)...

....

....

....

....

....

....

....

....

....

....

....

....

....

....

....

....

MY LISTS

List of the recommendations I have for my friends, family and others in the world

List of the traits of my doppelganger (my opposite or mythical evil twin) ....

....

....

....

....

....

....

....

....

....

....

....

....

....

....

....

....

....

List of the most important moments in history ....

....

....

....

....

....

....

....

....

....

....

....

....

....

....

....

....

....

....

List of the thank you notes I wish I had written, to whom and for why...

....

....

....

....

....

....

....

....

....

....

....

....

....

....

....

....

List of the questions I have always asked myself

MY LISTS

List of my heros

List of the wonders of the world, natural or man-made, according to me

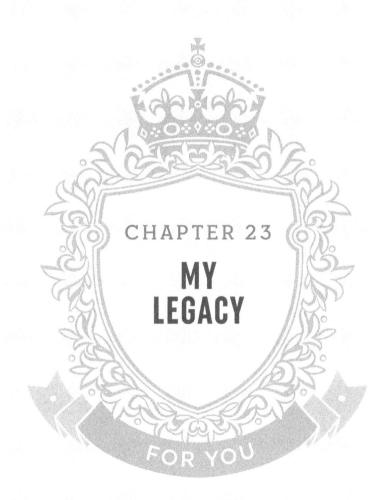

CHAPTER 23

MY
LEGACY

FOR YOU

MY LEGACY

How would I like to spend the last year of my life

....

....

....

....

....

How would I like to spend the last hour of my life

....

....

....

....

Who I would invite to my last supper

....

....

....

....

MY LEGACY

How I would like to be remembered in general ....

....

....

....

....

....

The most important things I ever did in my life ....

....

....

....

....

....

I believe I will go to heavan/hell because ....

....

....

....

....

....

....

MY LEGACY

What I think will happen after I die

....

....

....

....

....

What everyone needs to do to lead a life of the greatest meaning

....

....

....

....

....

Who I would like to speak at my funeral

....

....

....

....

....

MY LEGACY

How I prefer to be buried or cremated, and my wishes for my funeral ceremony............

....

....

....

....

....

The inscription I would want on my tombstone...

....

....

....

....

....

How I would like my family to remember me most..

....

....

....

....

....

MY LEGACY

Something that has always been on my mind

....

....

....

....

The one fantasy that I never fulfilled

....

....

....

....

The one lesson I hope I have taught others

....

....

....

....

MY LEGACY

The most cherished accomplishment in my life

....

....

....

....

....

....

....

....

The piece of wisdom I would pass along to a child

....

....

....

....

....

....

....

MY LEGACY

At my funeral,...

will tell the funniest story about me, and it will be about..

....

....

....

....

At my funeral,...

will tell the most touching story about me, and it will be about...

....

....

....

....

....

If I could ask my future self one question, that question would be...

....

....

....

MY LEGACY

Below I've shared some of what I would say at my own funderal if I could, in the form of a personal eulogy or a letter to myself.

MY LEGACY

More of my legacy ....

....

....

....

....

....

....

....

....

....

....

....

....

....

....

....

....

....

MY LEGACY

More of my legacy

CHAPTER 24

MY
STATS

FOR YOU

Name ....

Address ....

....

....

....

Phone ....

Email ....

My birthday ....

My birthplace ....

Birth hospital and physician's name ....

Birth moment details (type of birth, length of labor, complications) ....

....

....

....

My birth weight and length ....

How I describe myself as a baby ....

....

....

....

MY STATS

My corrective devices (glasses, braces, etc.) ....

....

Blood type ....

Allergies ....

....

Surgeries ....

....

....

....

Medical conditions ....

....

....

My overall health condition

....

....

....

....

....

MY STATS

The way I describe myself to doctors ....

MY STATS

My other stats

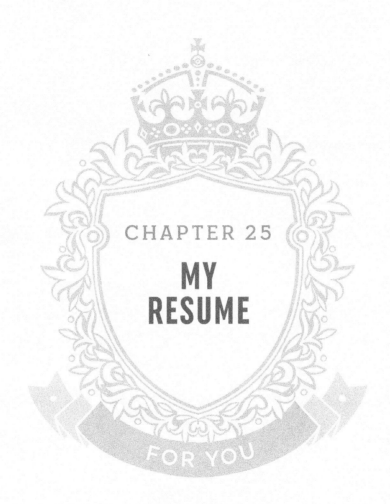

CHAPTER 25

MY
RESUME

FOR YOU

MY RESUME

HIGH SCHOOL

My High School (name, location, years) ....
....
....

My extracurricular activities, clubs or activities during school:

Special Memories

Orchestra	◯	
School plays	◯	
Band	◯	
Art	◯	
Crossing guard	◯	
Teacher's helper	◯	
Spelling bee	◯	
Math competition	◯	
Service club	◯	
Community service	◯	
Scouts (Boy/Girl scouts)	◯	
4-H	◯	
Music lessons	◯	
Karate	◯	
Special honors	◯	
Science fair	◯	

MY RESUME

Awards, contests or superlatives I won in high school

....

....

....

....

....

....

....

Sports and positions I played in high school

....

....

....

....

....

....

....

....

COLLEGE, TRADE AND ADVANCED DEGREES

College (name, location, years attended, degree, date granted)......................................

....

....

College (name, location, years attended, degree, date granted)......................................

....

....

College (name, location, years attended, degree, date granted)......................................

....

....

College (name, location, years attended, degree, date granted)......................................

....

....

College (name, location, years attended, degree, date granted)......................................

....

....

College activities, clubs or sports ....

....

....

....

....

....

....

ACCREDITATIONS

Professional associations, (name of certification, offices held, dates)...........................

....

....

....

....

....

....

....

MY RESUME

EMPLOYMENT

Job title ....

Company ....

Address ....

....

Start/end dates, ...

Primary responsibility ....

....

Pay ....

Job title ....

Company ....

Address ....

....

Start/end dates, ...

Primary responsibility ....

....

Pay ....

MY RESUME

Job title ....

Company ....

Address ....

....

Start/end dates, ...

Primary responsibility ....

....

Pay ....

_____

Job title ....

Company ....

Address ....

....

Start/end dates, ...

Primary responsibility ....

....

Pay ....

MY RESUME

Job title ....

Company ....

Address ....

....

Start/end dates, ...

Primary responsibility ....

....

Pay ....

Job title ....

Company ....

Address ....

....

Start/end dates, ...

Primary responsibility ....

....

Pay ....

MY RESUME

Job title ....

Company ....

Address ....

....

Start/end dates, ...

Primary responsibility ....

....

Pay ....

Job title ....

Company ....

Address ....

....

Start/end dates, ...

Primary responsibility ....

....

Pay ....

MY RESUME

Job title ....

Company ....

Address ....

....

Start/end dates, ...

Primary responsibility ....

....

Pay ....

Job title ....

Company ....

Address ....

....

Start/end dates, ...

Primary responsibility ....

....

Pay ....

MY RESUME

Job title ....

Company ....

Address ....

....

Start/end dates, ...

Primary responsibility ....

....

Pay ....

Job title ....

Company ....

Address ....

....

Start/end dates, ...

Primary responsibility ....

....

Pay ....

OTHER ROLES

Community or other organizations (years, positions held) ....

....

....

....

....

Awards and achievements, year and reason ....

....

....

....

....

The greatest achievement in my career was ....

....

....

....

....

MY RESUME

The greatest failure during my career was ....

....

....

....

....

Other noteworthy achievements in my career ....

....

....

....

....

I would describe my career as ....

....

....

....

....

....

....

....

....

MY RESUME

My professional biography in a short paragraph

Work stories or moments

....

....

....

....

....

....

....

....

....

....

....

....

....

....

....

....

....

....

CHAPTER 26

MY
PARENTS

FOR YOU

MY PARENTS

MY FATHER

Name...

Birthday...

Place of Birth..

 Lives in...

or passed away on...

My father's religious denomination and views...

....

My father grew up in...

My father described his childhood as...

....

....

....

My father's siblings (name, birthdate, deathdate, spouse, children)....................

....

....

....

....

MY PARENTS

My father was educated at ....

My father's marriages (spouse name, place and date of ceremony, if ended, date and how) ...

....

....

....

....

....

My father was named after ....

My father's health ....

....

....

....

....

....

....

....

....

....

....

MY FATHER'S PARENTS

My grandmother's name ....

Maiden name ....

Nationality ....

Race ....

Ethnicity ....

Birth date/location ....

Death date/ocation ....

My grandfather's name ....

Nationality ....

Race ....

Ethnicity ....

Birth date/location ....

Death date/ocation ....

MY PARENTS

Special father memories

MY PARENTS

MY MOTHER

Name ....

Birthday ....

Place of Birth ....

Lives in ....

or passed away on ....

My mother's religious denomination and views ....

....

My mother grew up in ....

My mother described her childhood as ....

....

....

....

My mothers siblings (name, birthdate, deathdate, spouse, children) ....

....

....

....

....

....

MY PARENTS

My mother was educated at ....

My mother's marriages (spouse name, place and date of ceremony, if ended, date and how) .

....

....

....

....

....

My mother was named after ....

My mother's health ....

....

....

....

....

....

....

....

....

....

....

MY MOTHER'S PARENTS

My grandmother's name ....

Maiden name ....

Nationality ....

Race ....

Ethnicity ....

Birth date/location ....

Death date/ocation ....

My grandfather's name ....

Nationality ....

Race ....

Ethnicity ....

Birth date/location ....

Death date/ocation ....

MY PARENTS

Special mother memories

CPSIA information can be obtained
at www.ICGtesting.com
Printed in the USA
BVHW011406060721
611233BV00003B/621